THE BOOK OF WEALTH

The Book of Wealth

ISBN (*paperback*): 979-8-9922899-0-9
ISBN (*ebook*): 979-8-9922899-1-6
ISBN (*audiobook*): 979-8-9922899-2-3

Editorial services: Sandra Wendel, Write On, Inc.
Design: Marko Markovic, 5mediadesign.com

Published by ClearValue Tax (visit on YouTube)
Contact the author at www.clearvalueinvesting.com

THE BOOK OF WEALTH

10 STEPS TO FINANCIAL FREEDOM

BRIAN KIM

CONTENTS

BRIAN'S PROMISE:

GUIDING YOU TO FINANCIAL FREEDOM

Have you ever wondered why so many hardworking people struggle to achieve wealth, even when they save diligently and follow all the advice they've been given?

It's not a lack of ambition or intelligence that holds them back. The truth is, they've never been given clear, practical instructions on how to build wealth.

But here's the good news—with the right guidance, financial prosperity becomes attainable.

Let me explain with a simple analogy.

Imagine I asked you to bake a delicious apple pie without a recipe. You probably know most of the ingredients: apples, pie crust, sugar, butter. But without clear instructions, turning those ingredients into a satisfying pie would be difficult.

Building wealth is no different. There's a process to follow.

If you've been struggling financially, it's likely because you don't have the right instructions. Many of us know some of the elements—hard work, budgeting, investing—but without knowing how to combine them effectively, we struggle to build wealth.

I'm here to make that easier for you.

In this book, I'll give you a simple, step-by-step recipe for building wealth. These strategies transformed my life, and they can do the same for you.

With the right guidance, you'll see that building wealth is not just possible—it's straightforward.

My name is Brian, and if you follow me on social media, you might already know me. I'm fortunate to have millions of subscribers who trust me for financial advice. As a financial educator, my mission is simple: to help people like you achieve financial freedom.

If you're familiar with my work, you know that I'm direct, straightforward, and I don't sugarcoat things. Here's what you can always expect from me:

- **I'm here to help you.**
- **I'll give you the truth, no matter how hard it may be to hear.**
- **I value your time and won't waste it.**
- **I'll guide you step by step on the path to becoming wealthy and financially free.**

I'm on your side, and I'm rooting for your success every step of the way.

WHY YOU'RE CAPABLE: MY BELIEF IN YOUR SUCCESS

I believe you and I share similar values and goals because you're here seeking ways to improve your life and achieve financial freedom—just like I once did. If we met in person, I know we'd get along well. That's why I already see you as both a friend and an ally.

I'm writing this book with the intention of sharing valuable insights with someone I genuinely care about because I do care about you. My goal is to help you achieve success, freedom, and fulfillment.

And let me assure you: you are more than capable.

If you've made it this far and feel a connection with what I'm saying, then you are ready to take the next steps.

It's really that simple, and soon you'll see for yourself.

1

THE WEALTH-BUILDING FORMULA

I used to think wealth was reserved for the lucky or privileged—something you were born into or stumbled upon by chance. That belief changed when I discovered a simple formula that transformed my financial life.

In the beginning, I was overwhelmed by the constant stress of living paycheck to paycheck. It felt like no matter how hard I worked, financial freedom was always just out of reach.

Determined to find a better way, I faced trial and error and made plenty of mistakes. Though frustrating at times, these experiences ultimately helped me uncover a straightforward approach that turned my financial struggles into lasting prosperity.

THE SIMPLE STEPS TO WEALTH

Step 1: Earn more than you spend.

Step 2: Invest the surplus.

Step 3: Protect your money from loss.

Step 4: Repeat these steps.

TAKE CONTROL OF YOUR FINANCIAL FUTURE

When I first applied these steps, the results weren't instant, but after a few months, I saw real financial progress.

Now, let's dive into the steps that will accelerate your wealth-building journey.

2

HOW TO ACCELERATE YOUR WEALTH CREATION

What if I told you that the fastest way to build wealth isn't through extreme frugality or chasing the next big investment?

Many people believe that cutting expenses is the key to financial freedom. While important, it's only one part of the equation.

Here's the real game changer: You can only cut so much, but there's virtually no limit to how much you can earn. Your potential for wealth grows significantly when you focus on boosting your income.

Growing your wealth is based on this simple formula:

Income – Expenses = Surplus (or Deficit)

Reducing expenses helps, but increasing your income amplifies your surplus. To accelerate wealth-building, focusing on income growth is essential.

I learned this the hard way. Early on, I chased quick wins through risky investments, hoping to leapfrog to wealth. Those efforts backfired, wasting valuable time.

START WITH LIMITED RESOURCES

You may be thinking:

- **I don't have a lot of money.**
- **I don't make a lot of money.**

If you had more money, it'd be easier to build wealth, right? A higher-paying job would make things simpler, wouldn't it?

If you find yourself without either, I get it—I've been there.

I understand the struggle, stress, and frustration. It's exhausting and can feel like you're stuck.

Fortunately, you don't have to stay trapped. When I shifted my focus to increasing my income, everything changed. Learn from my mistakes and fast-track your journey to financial freedom.

MY MISTAKE OF CHASING FAST MONEY

In my twenties, I was earning a mediocre income working for a large company. I believed there was no way I could become wealthy on a modest salary. Without clear guidance on wealth-building, I turned to the stock market as a shortcut, convinced that big gains were the best path to financial freedom.

At the time, I thought I was investing, but in reality, I was speculating. My goal wasn't steady growth—I wanted to turn \$1,000 into \$100,000. I spent countless hours researching stocks, analyzing financials, tracking market trends, and constantly monitoring my portfolio. It felt like a second job, but I believed it was worth it because I had some early wins.

I was chasing the idea of getting rich quickly, not building sustainable wealth. I wasn't investing for the long term. I was gambling, hoping for life-changing returns with each pick. This mindset led me to waste time and energy on speculative strategies that didn't pay off in the end.

ROUND 1: MY FIRST TASTE OF FAST MONEY IN STOCKS

I turned \$1,000 into \$50,000 on a risky penny stock. I bought in at the right time, sold near the peak, and felt incredibly talented. Naturally, I thought I could do it again.

I took my \$50,000 and bought another penny stock, aiming for a million dollars. But the stock plummeted, and

I lost most of my money. The euphoria quickly faded as my gains evaporated.

I realized I had been naive. That win was more luck than skill, and I let greed take over as I chased bigger payoffs.

ROUND 2: A BIG WIN WITH STOCK OPTIONS

A few years later, I turned $1,000 into $60,000 using call options. Watching my profits skyrocket was an exhilarating rush, and it fueled my confidence that the stock could climb even higher over the next day or two, so I held off on selling.

But the next day, bad news emerged about the company, and the stock plummeted along with my call options. In a matter of hours, most of my gains were gone. Looking back, I should have sold sooner, but I was completely blindsided—who could have predicted a company scandal?

This experience taught me that black swan events—those unpredictable, rare events—can strike anytime, and no amount of research can fully prepare you for them.

ROUND 3: A BIG WIN IN CRYPTO

Years later, I invested $2,000 into a cryptocurrency that surged to $20,000. Feeling nervous but satisfied with a 10x return, I sold it.

However, the cryptocurrency kept rising, eventually reaching 100x gains. In hindsight, I sold too early and missed an even bigger opportunity. As the price climbed higher, I couldn't shake the lingering regret of selling too soon.

This taught me that consistently timing the market with precision is incredibly difficult—if not impossible.

REFLECTING ON SPECULATION

I found a few winners over the years, but speculating didn't help me make real progress toward building wealth. It was mentally exhausting. I spent hours researching, analyzing, and stressing, with little to show for it.

I began asking myself: Why am I doing this? Why am I clinging to a strategy that clearly isn't working? After some deep self-reflection, I realized I held onto speculation because it felt like my only hope for wealth and freedom. If I let go, what did I have left?

That's when I realized I was behaving like someone playing the lottery—knowing the odds but driven by hope. I was betting on long shots, fully aware of how unlikely they were to pay off.

That's when I decided to stop leaving my financial future to chance. I wasn't going to rely on speculation anymore. No more chasing quick wins. I needed a solid, sustainable plan for true financial freedom.

THE PIVOT: FROM SPECULATING TO INVESTING

Tired of the constant ups and downs, I shifted from speculation to investing. I focused on picking value stocks, diversifying, and aiming for steady growth. For a few years, I even outperformed the market.

But then another problem became clear. Even if I realized a 20% return, while good on paper, it wasn't life-changing. For example, if you have $40,000 and make 20%, that's $8,000—a nice amount, but not transformative.

At that point, I asked myself: Why am I spending twenty hours a week managing and stressing over my portfolio for an extra $8,000 a year? When I did the math, I realized I could have earned more by simply taking on a part-time job. The time and effort weren't worth the reward.

That's when I knew I needed a new approach. While investing was less risky than speculating, it wasn't creating the wealth I wanted. The problem wasn't the strategy—it was the scale. I needed to focus on increasing my income, so I could invest more and truly benefit from compounding.

This became my new focus. I stopped seeing investing as my primary wealth-building strategy and started viewing it as part of a bigger plan. The more I earned, the more I could invest, and only then would those returns make a real difference.

MY ADVICE IF YOU DON'T HAVE A LOT OF MONEY TO INVEST

Your active income—the money you earn from working—fuels wealth-building in the early stages. The more you earn, the more you can invest, which amplifies returns. That's why increasing your income should be your main focus initially.

If you're just starting out, prioritize learning the basics of stock market investing. This foundation will help you in the future. There's no need to spend too much time analyzing individual stocks or chasing passive income streams right now. Those strategies come later.

Early on, your investments should focus on stability and consistent returns with minimal effort. A well-diversified index fund or ETF is ideal, freeing you to concentrate on what matters: growing your income so you can invest and build wealth.

DIFFERENT PATHS TO WEALTH: FIND WHAT WORKS FOR YOU

Whether you're an employee or self-employed, wealth and financial freedom are achievable. Not everyone is suited for self-employment, and that's perfectly fine. There's no single "right way" to reach financial freedom. Your path may differ from someone else's.

Think of it like this:

1 + 9 = 10
2 + 8 = 10
3 + 7 = 10

There's more than one way to get the job done. The key is to find what works for you based on your strengths and goals.

PRACTICAL STRATEGIES TO BOOST YOUR INCOME

Here are several ways to increase your income:

- **Increase your compensation for your skills:**
  - **Employees:** Climb the corporate ladder and negotiate raises.
  - **Self-employed:** Raise your prices to reflect your value.
- **Take on additional work:**
  - **Employees:** Consider overtime, a part-time job, or a side hustle.
  - **Self-employed:** Extend hours or improve processes to increase output.
- **Seek higher-paying opportunities:**
  - **Employees:** Switch companies or move into a higher-paying industry.
  - **Self-employed:** Pivot to a product or service with higher earning potential.

COMMIT TO YOUR FIELD AND MASTER IT

To significantly increase your income, commit to one field and become an expert. Reaching the top of your field allows you to command a higher level of compensation.

Top performers consistently earn much more than those who are just "good." For example, a top accountant can earn up to twenty times more than the average one. The same applies to other fields—celebrity chefs earn much more than average chefs due to their expertise and reputation.

Mastery doesn't limit you; it opens doors. You can leverage your expertise to branch into new areas, further boosting your income. Master your field, and the market will reward you.

HOW TO BECOME AN EXPERT

Becoming an expert requires a strong commitment to learning, practicing, and gaining experience. How quickly you reach expert status depends on two key factors:

1. **The effort you're willing to put in.**
2. **The time you dedicate to mastering your craft.**

The more you invest in your growth, the faster you'll see results in developing expertise. In the next section, we'll dive deeper into how effort and time shape this journey.

THE EFFORT

Let's say you're working forty hours a week. You have two choices:

Option A: Do the bare minimum to avoid getting fired. In this case, you won't develop new skills quickly, and your progress will be slow.

Option B: Fully engage with your work. Actively seek ways to expand your expertise, take on challenges, and deepen your knowledge. This accelerates your growth and development.

Either way, you're working those forty hours, so why not make the most of it? If you choose Option B, you'll improve your skills much faster. The effort you put in is entirely up to you—that drive must come from within.

That's why it's crucial to choose a field or job you enjoy or at least don't mind. When you're in an area that plays to your strengths, putting in the effort becomes easier. But if you're stuck in a job that makes you miserable, it'll be hard to stay motivated.

THE TIME

Time is just as important as effort. Imagine two financial analysts that put in the same amount of effort:

- **Scenario A: two years of experience**
- **Scenario B: ten years of experience**

Which one has a stronger understanding of financial markets? Clearly, Scenario B. More time leads to deeper insights and valuable knowledge that can't be gained overnight.

And which scenario leads to higher income? Again, Scenario B. With time comes expertise, bigger opportunities, and higher-profile assignments.

The time you spend in your field is an investment, and how you use that time determines your success. If you want to increase your income, becoming an expert is key. Expertise takes time and effort, so it's important to choose a field you can commit to for the long term. As your experience grows, so will your value, and that will be reflected in your earnings.

DON'T BE LIKE MY FRIEND: THE JACK-OF-ALL-TRADES

This is a true story, and I learned a lot from it.

My friend and I studied accounting together in college. We worked on group projects, got similar grades, and started our careers as accountants.

We graduated at the same time, and he started his career as an accountant, just like me. However, our futures took very different paths.

After working as an accountant for four years, he thought he could make fast money in real estate. He told me, "That's where the money's at!"

Eager to get rich quickly, he quit his accounting job to become a real estate agent, starting from scratch with no clients.

Despite his enthusiasm, after four years in real estate, he ended up with an income similar to his accounting job. His plan of making a lot of money very quickly did not happen.

Convinced that marketing was a more lucrative industry, he decided to switch careers again. He landed a position as a marketing specialist at a big agency but started at the bottom with entry-level pay.

Yet again, after four more years, his income remained similar to when he was an accountant.

He contemplated changing to a new industry once more.

My friend never stayed in one field long enough to become an expert. He ended up mediocre in several disciplines, which is why his compensation stayed mediocre. Twelve years after we graduated, he was about to start over in another new field.

If he had just stuck with any of those professions from the start, he could have been making a substantial income within those twelve years.

Consider this:

- **Real estate is lucrative.**
- **Marketing is lucrative.**
- **Accounting is lucrative.**

All of these fields can be highly rewarding if you become an expert.

THE DANGER OF SWITCHING CAREERS

Switching to an unrelated field often means starting over as a beginner, which can delay your progress and income.

If you're in a dead-end job or miserable, changing careers might be necessary. I understand why you might consider the setback worth it, but it's important to be mindful of the consequences and make a thoughtful decision. I just want to ensure you're fully aware of the potential impact and approach this choice with care.

That's why it's important to identify your goals early on, so you can avoid wasting time. My advice: choose a career you won't resent. If you're unhappy, you'll eventually want to leave it.

Additionally, choose a field where top performers earn an income you'd be satisfied with. While reaching the top isn't guaranteed, the potential should be worth pursuing.

By sticking with one field and becoming an expert, you boost your chances of real financial success. Don't scatter your efforts chasing quick wealth.

THE MISSING LINK: VISIBILITY AND INCOME GROWTH

Becoming an expert is crucial for building wealth, but expertise alone won't maximize your income. The next step is monetizing your skills effectively—and that requires visibility.

People need to know you exist and understand the value you bring. Without visibility, your expertise goes unnoticed, and you miss out on the financial rewards you deserve. Let me share my experience.

I had my own tax practice and was confident that I was the best tax accountant in my area for my target market. I had deeper knowledge, better service, and lower rates than most competitors. Yet, my business wasn't booming. Why? I lacked visibility.

But over time, something started to shift when satisfied clients left online reviews. As more reviews accumulated, my visibility grew. Soon, I became the top-ranked independent tax provider in my area. Demand skyrocketed, allowing me to raise rates, hire staff, and expand my business—all because I increased my visibility.

How can you do the same? Here are practical steps to get noticed and show the value of your expertise:

- **Leverage online platforms and social media:** Showcase your skills and connect with others in your field.
- **Network within your industry:** Attend conferences, webinars, or meetups to interact with peers and potential clients.

- **Ask for recommendations:** Encourage satisfied colleagues, clients, or supervisors to endorse your skills through reviews or spreading the word.

Don't just be the best—make sure people know it. By building an online presence, networking, and showcasing your work, you'll unlock greater opportunities and income.

INCREASE YOUR VISIBILITY AS AN EMPLOYEE

Visibility isn't just important for entrepreneurs—it's equally critical for employees aiming to advance their careers and boost income. Here are strategies to increase visibility and unlock new opportunities as an employee:

Start by networking within your industry, connecting with recruiters, and actively searching for job openings. The more visible you are, the greater your opportunities for advancement. If a new employer offers a higher salary, seize the opportunity if it fits, or use that job offer to negotiate a raise at your current company.

If you're considering a job switch, secure a new position before leaving your current one to maintain financial security.

Another key factor to consider is expanding your geographical reach, which can significantly boost your income. Limiting your job search to your city or state restricts both your visibility and earning potential, while employers in other regions may offer substantially higher compensation for your expertise.

If you're an expert, offers locally will be solid, but looking beyond your immediate area can reveal employers who highly value your skills and are willing to pay top dollar.

Naturally, relocating is a significant decision that requires careful consideration of factors such as cost of living, family, and lifestyle. But by broadening your search, you open up more opportunities.

Expanding your network, job offers, and geographical reach can result in far greater rewards than you initially imagined.

WHAT WE KNOW

If you're not earning a high income or don't have much to invest, avoid getting sidetracked by shortcuts that promise quick wealth. While learning the basics of investing is important, chasing fast money often leads to frustration and wasted effort.

Right now, your focus should be on increasing your income. The formula is simple: The more you earn, the more you can invest, and the faster you can build lasting wealth. Manage your expenses wisely and let your rising income power your investments.

3

HOW TO ACHIEVE CONSISTENT WEALTH GROWTH

I have an important question for you:

Are you currently

- **Destroying your wealth?**
- **Stuck and going nowhere?**
- **Growing your wealth?**

Right now, you're doing one of these three things—whether you're aware of it or not. But which one is it?

Take a moment to reflect on your financial habits. Are you actively building wealth, or could you be unintentionally sabotaging your future? Be honest with yourself.

It's easy to feel stuck or frustrated, especially when you're putting in the effort but not seeing the results you expect. The key is recognizing where you truly stand, so let's figure it out together.

HOW TO DESTROY YOUR WEALTH

The formula for destroying wealth is simple: Spend more than you make. You can do this by

- **Dipping into your savings**
- **Selling assets to fund overspending**
- **Going into debt to finance a lifestyle you can't afford**

It may feel like you're just covering life's essentials, but if you consistently spend more than you make—even on stuff that seems necessary—you're creating a financial hole that's hard to escape. I've seen countless hardworking people fall into this trap, often realizing the damage only when it's too late.

HOW TO STAY STUCK AND GO NOWHERE

The formula for staying stuck is simple: Spend exactly what you make. While you won't be losing money, you won't be building wealth either. You'll remain in the same spot, living paycheck to paycheck. It's like running on a financial treadmill. You're working hard but not moving forward.

Take a moment to reflect: Do you find yourself working just to cover your bills, with nothing left at the end of the month? You're not alone—many people share this frustration. The first step toward change is creating a financial surplus.

HOW TO GROW YOUR WEALTH

The key to growing wealth is simple: Spend less than you make.

The surplus between your income and expenses can be used to

- **Save**
- **Invest in assets that grow over time**

This is the path to financial freedom, and the best part is that anyone can follow it, regardless of their current circumstances. You don't need a high income or a lucky investment break. What you need is a surplus, and I'll show you how to create it.

A PROVEN BLUEPRINT FOR BUILDING WEALTH

Let me guide you through the steps that helped me put this plan into action successfully.

STEP 1: TRACK YOUR MONEY

To spend less than you make, you need to know two key factors:

- **How much you're making.**
- **How much you're spending.**

This isn't about creating a budget. It's an accounting of your money. You need a clear, detailed picture of exactly where your money is going. No rough estimates or guesswork; it must be accurate and written down.

Practical Tip: I personally track my income and expenses with a simple spreadsheet. It's free, straightforward, and works.

If you prefer using an app or specialized software, go for it. The method doesn't matter as long as it's something you'll stick with.

I recommend tracking on a monthly basis. Why monthly? Because the goal is to create a surplus each month—and consistency is key.

Example: Let's say your monthly income after taxes is $4,000, and you're spending $3,500. That leaves you with a $500 surplus. Here's how your spending might break down:

- **Housing: $1,300**
- **Groceries: $650**
- **Transportation: $500**
- **Insurance: $400**

- **Utilities: $300**
- **Entertainment: $250**
- **Miscellaneous: $100**

By categorizing your expenses, you can see exactly where your money is going and easily spot areas where you can make adjustments.

Take a moment to reflect: Think about your own finances for a minute. Do you have a clear picture of where your money is going? If not, take some time to list out your income and expenses. The more precise you are, the better you'll understand your financial health.

TRACKING YOUR INCOME

Make sure to track your monthly income after taxes. Your gross income is less important—it's what actually lands in your bank account that matters.

TRACKING YOUR SPENDING

Organize your spending into clear categories. The goal is to answer two key questions:

- **How much are you spending?**
- **What are you spending it on?**

Detailed categories will give you a complete picture and help you identify where you may be overspending.

STEP 2: ANALYZE YOUR RESULTS

Now that you've tracked your income and expenses, it's time to review your results.

Are you consistently generating a surplus?

- **If yes, great! You're building wealth.**
- **If not, don't panic. Now you know where you stand, and that's the first step toward progress.**

STEP 3: MAKE IMPROVEMENTS

Now comes the crucial step: making adjustments.

Even if you already have a surplus, there's always room to accelerate your wealth-building. If you're in a deficit, your focus should be on closing that gap and moving toward a surplus.

Wealth-building is a marathon, not a sprint. You don't need to cut every indulgence or make drastic changes overnight. Start with small, manageable improvements each month. Steady, consistent progress—no matter how small—will get you to where you want to be.

HOW TO SHRINK YOUR DEFICIT OR INCREASE YOUR SURPLUS

If you're unsure where to begin, here are some practical steps that worked for me:

- **Eliminate wasted expenses:** Start by canceling small, automatic payments like unnecessary memberships or subscriptions. How many do you really use? Cut anything that doesn't add value to your life. This is an easy way to stop unnecessary spending.
- **Cut back on excessive spending:** I used to spend too much dining out. Cooking at home saved money and was healthier. Pick one area where you're overspending—whether it's eating out, shopping, or something else—and scale back. Start small; over time, these adjustments add up.
- **Find less expensive alternatives:** Look for better deals on major expenses like insurance. I switched providers and found cheaper, better coverage. Review your bills and see where you can save.
- **Become a smart shopper:** Purchase in bulk when practical, and take advantage of promotions or seasonal discounts. These small savings can accumulate significantly over time.

A PERSONAL STORY: MY WAKE-UP CALL

At one point, I thought I had my finances under control. I had a decent salary and didn't think I was overspending. But the day I tracked my spending for the first time, I had a major reality check.

I discovered that a significant part of my income was being drained by things that added no real value—impulsive online purchases, unused memberships, and frequently dining out. These were small, everyday expenses, but over time, they were quietly eating away at my finances.

It wasn't easy to accept how much I was wasting, but that moment was a turning point. I started making small changes: cutting out impulse buys, reducing how often I ate out, and canceling unused subscriptions. These adjustments didn't feel like sacrifices; they felt like taking back control. Within a few months, I was consistently generating a surplus, and that's when my wealth truly began to grow.

The lesson? Often, it's the unnoticed, everyday expenses that hold you back. But once you track your money, you can see where you're losing and make the changes to start winning.

MY VIEW ON BUDGETING

While I believe budgeting is optional, accounting for your money is necessary.

For larger purchases, such as a vehicle or property, I set a budget with a spending limit. But for day-to-day expenses, I don't follow a rigid budget. Instead, I focus on living within my means and avoid unnecessary spending.

I stay accountable with a monthly financial check-up. This gives me a clear picture of whether I'm staying on track or slipping into a deficit. The numbers don't lie, and they keep me in check.

WHY I PREFER ACCOUNTING OVER BUDGETING

Rigid budgets can feel restrictive, almost like punishing yourself for spending on things you enjoy. That's why I prefer tracking and accounting. It's not about deprivation—it's about knowing where your money goes and making mindful decisions. With a flexible approach, it's easier to stay on course without feeling overwhelmed.

TURNING HABITS INTO WEALTH

By tracking your money, analyzing your results, and making improvements, you'll be on the path to building wealth. The steps are simple, but the execution is where many people fall short. Stick with it, and over time, you'll see the benefits in your financial health.

Remember, the longer you wait to address your finances, the harder it becomes to break bad habits. Start today—even if it's just writing down your income and expenses. Every small step moves you closer to your financial goals.

4

HOW TO INVEST PROPERLY

To build wealth, you must put your money to work. Investing is the engine that powers your financial growth, which allows you to earn more money from what you already have. However, while investing can be incredibly powerful, there's a right way to do it—and certainly a wrong way.

The key to successful investing is understanding its true purpose: to grow your money safely and steadily over time. While the idea of quick gains can be tempting, it's crucial to approach investing with a long-term, defensive mindset.

THE PROPER WAY TO INVEST

Investing is about growing wealth slowly and securely. While it may seem less exciting than chasing high returns, this approach minimizes the risk of losing money. The quickest way to destroy wealth is by taking unnecessary risks in pursuit of outsized gains.

To accelerate your wealth-building, the best strategy is simple: increase your income and invest more money. This ensures steady growth without jeopardizing your financial security. The more money you can invest safely, the faster your wealth will compound over time.

Never put your financial future at risk by chasing risky high returns. Losing money is counterproductive. Instead, focus on reliable, conservative investments that offer consistent growth over time.

BEWARE OF SPECULATIVE INVESTMENTS

Speculating on high-risk, high-reward opportunities can be tempting, especially when the potential payoff seems significant. But relying on speculation to build wealth is like depending on winning the lottery to achieve financial freedom.

I made this mistake early on when I was chasing penny stocks in hopes of life-changing returns. While I did have a few big wins, the losses were just as devastating, slowing my progress toward financial freedom. I was playing a risky game that ultimately delayed my wealth-building journey.

It's okay to engage in speculative investments occasionally, but do so in moderation. If you decide to speculate, only use a small portion of your portfolio—that would be money you can afford to lose without jeopardizing your financial goals.

THE POWER OF COMPOUND GROWTH

One of the greatest benefits of steady investing is the power of compound growth. Initially, progress may seem slow, but as your investments grow, they generate returns on previous returns and thus accelerate your wealth exponentially.

Consider this example: If you start with a penny that doubles every day for thirty days, it grows from $0.01 to over $5 million. That's the power of compounding. It starts slowly, but with time, the growth becomes exponential:

- **Day 1: $0.01**
- **Day 2: $0.02**
- **Day 3: $0.04**
- **Day 4: $0.08**
- **Day 5: $0.16**
- **Day 6: $0.32**
- **Day 7: $0.64**
- **Day 8: $1.28**

- **Day 9: $2.56**
- **Day 10: $5.12**
- **Day 11: $10.24**
- **Day 12: $20.48**
- **Day 13: $40.96**
- **Day 14: $81.92**
- **Day 15: $163.84**
- **Day 16: $327.68**
- **Day 17: $655.36**
- **Day 18: $1,310.72**
- **Day 19: $2,621.44**
- **Day 20: $5,242.88**
- **Day 21: $10,485.76**
- **Day 22: $20,971.52**
- **Day 23: $41,943.04**
- **Day 24: $83,886.08**
- **Day 25: $167,772.16**
- **Day 26: $335,544.32**
- **Day 27: $671,088.64**
- **Day 28: $1,342,177.28**
- **Day 29: $2,684,354.56**
- **Day 30: $5,368,709.12**

Time is your greatest ally in harnessing the power of compound growth. The earlier you start investing, the more time your money has to grow. Even small contributions made consistently can lead to substantial wealth over time.

THE PROCESS OF INVESTING AND GROWING YOUR WEALTH

Building wealth through investing takes consistency and patience. The process is straightforward:

- **Spend less than you make, so you have money left over to invest.**
- **Consistently add to your investments every month, even if it's a small amount.**
- **Allow your money to grow by keeping it invested without withdrawing.**

Treat your investments as off-limits until you reach financial freedom. Dipping into your investment accounts for unnecessary spending or emergencies will only slow your progress. Withdraw only when you've reached your financial goals.

CONSERVATIVE INVESTMENT OPTIONS

When seeking conservative investments, prioritize stability and long-term growth. Here are a few reliable options:

- **Index funds and ETFs:** These track a market index, such as the S&P 500, offering diversification and reduced risk. For example, investing in an S&P 500 index fund means you're buying a broad mix of top US companies, which lowers risk while supporting long-term growth.
- **Bonds:** Bonds are fixed-income investments where you lend money to a corporation or government in

exchange for interest payments. They typically offer more safety than stocks but with lower returns.

- **Real estate:** Thoughtfully investing in real estate can provide both rental income and property appreciation. Whether residential or commercial, real estate can be a stable option for conservative investors.

The key is to diversify your investments across different asset classes, which helps minimize risk and support steady growth over time.

TAKE ACTION AND BUILD YOUR FUTURE

The key to building wealth is consistency. By taking small, steady steps today, you set yourself up for exponential growth in the future. Building wealth isn't just about making the right financial decisions—it's about committing to the process, trusting in time, and taking action today.

5

ESCAPE THE DEBT TRAP

Debt can feel like an overwhelming burden that is holding you back from reaching your goals and achieving financial freedom. Debt doesn't have to define or control your life. With the right strategy, you can lift that burden, take control of your finances, and reclaim your financial freedom.

ELIMINATE DEBT AND REGAIN CONTROL

While avoiding debt altogether is ideal, I understand that for most of us, that's not always realistic. Like many people, I've carried debt at different stages of my life—whether it was an auto loan, a mortgage, or credit card debt. But I made it a priority to pay off those debts as quickly as possible.

Here's a step-by-step process to help you eliminate your debt and regain your financial freedom:

STEP 1: EXPLORE OPPORTUNITIES TO ELIMINATE DEBT WITHOUT PAYING IT ALL OFF

Before making payments, explore legal or strategic options to reduce or even eliminate your debt.

- **Example**: Government programs may forgive student loans if you work in public service for a certain number of years. Consider whether this aligns with your career goals and if it's worth pursuing.
- **Example**: Declaring bankruptcy may eliminate some debts, like credit card balances, but carefully weigh the long-term financial consequences before making this decision.

STEP 2: LOWER YOUR INTEREST RATES

If you can't eliminate the debt, the next best step is to lower the interest rates you're paying.

- **Example:** Refinancing your mortgage could lower your interest rate and reduce your monthly payments, but make sure to account for closing costs and determine whether the long-term savings justify any expenses.

STEP 3: PRIORITIZE HIGH-INTEREST DEBT FIRST

When paying off your debt, focus on high-interest balances first. High-interest debt, like credit cards, compounds quickly and can erode your financial progress.

- **Example:** If you have credit card debt with a 20% interest rate and an auto loan at 7%, prioritize the credit card debt. Pay it off first.

STEP 4: PAY MORE THAN THE MINIMUM

Paying only the minimum on your debt keeps you trapped in the cycle far longer than necessary. To make real progress, pay more than the minimum required.

- **Set realistic goals for how quickly you want to pay off your debt.** Don't be too aggressive—you still need enough cash for everyday expenses and emergencies. Stressing yourself out by putting every penny toward debt is counterproductive. As long as you're consistently paying more than the minimum, you're accelerating your progress.

IS ALL DEBT BAD?

It's a common question: Is borrowing money ever a good idea if it can help you make more money? Is all debt bad?

- **Example:** If you can borrow money at a 3% interest rate and invest it in an opportunity that yields an 8% return, is that a smart move?
- **Or should you pay off a mortgage with a low interest rate of 3%,** or invest that money in the stock market where you could potentially earn 8 to 12%?

My answer is this: Yes, debt is inherently bad because it represents a liability. However, if the benefits outweigh the drawbacks, using debt as a financial tool can make sense. The key is fully understanding the risks involved.

AN ANALOGY: DEBT IS LIKE GETTING PUNCHED

Think of it this way: Is getting punched in the stomach bad? Of course. But what if someone offered you a billion dollars to take that punch? You might decide it's worth it. That doesn't change the fact that getting punched is bad. It just means that in this case, the benefits outweigh the drawbacks.

Debt works the same way. It's always bad, but if you determine that it's worth it and you can manage the risk, then don't be afraid to use debt to your advantage. Just be cautious, and never take on more debt than you can handle because things don't always go as planned.

DON'T LET DEBT GROW: ACT NOW

The longer you wait to address your debt, the harder it becomes to overcome. High-interest debt, like credit cards, can accumulate quickly, making it increasingly difficult to catch up. With each month you delay, interest compounds, and the debt grows larger. This not only slows your path toward financial freedom but also limits your ability to invest and build wealth.

Start today. Whether it's reviewing your debt, negotiating better terms, or paying off high-interest balances, every step you take moves you closer to financial freedom.

BEWARE OF LIFESTYLE INFLATION

When your income increases, it's tempting to justify spending more. After all, you've worked hard, and it's natural to want to enjoy the rewards. But be cautious of lifestyle inflation—that's the habit of increasing your spending as your income grows.

While lifestyle inflation can feel gratifying in the short term, over time, it can trap you in a cycle where, despite earning more, you aren't making real progress toward financial freedom. As you raise your standard of living, your expenses—whether in the form of car loans, mortgage payments, or credit card balances—can rise just as quickly. Before long, any extra income you've earned is being absorbed by new expenses.

I've seen many people fall into this cycle, and the longer it goes on, the harder it is to break free. You might feel as if you're doing better financially because your income has grown, but if your spending rises at the same rate, your financial situation stays the same. The key is to keep your spending under control as your income increases, so you can use that additional money to pay down debt or invest for your future.

THE MOMENT I RECLAIMED MY FREEDOM

I still remember the day I made my last debt payment. It wasn't just about the numbers. No, it felt like I was reclaiming control of my life. The stress melted away, and I realized that from that moment forward, every dollar I earned was truly mine to build a better future. That's the kind of freedom I want you to experience as well.

6

PROTECT YOUR WEALTH FROM SETBACKS

Building wealth isn't just about increasing your income—it's about safeguarding what you've earned from the inevitable challenges that threaten to take it away.

Financial setbacks can strike without warning, whether through stock market crashes, economic downturns, or personal emergencies. While these events can be frustrating and discouraging, setbacks are a natural part of the journey. What truly matters is how you prepare for and respond to them, ensuring they don't derail your progress.

In this chapter, I'll share my own experiences with financial challenges and the key lessons I've learned along the way. These insights will help you minimize risk and protect the wealth you've worked hard to build.

STOCK MARKET CRASHES ARE INEVITABLE

Market crashes are an inevitable part of investing, but they don't have to disrupt your long-term strategy. It's natural to feel anxious when markets fall, but selling out of panic or fear only locks in losses. Instead, focus on diversifying your portfolio across different sectors to reduce risk and soften the impact of downturns. By holding high-quality stocks and practicing patience, you'll be better positioned to weather the storm and benefit from the eventual recovery.

Take the 2020 stock market crash during the pandemic as an example. Many investors panicked and sold off their holdings, locking in their losses. However, those who stayed the course and held on saw their portfolios recover and even grow within a few months. Historically, the stock market has always recovered from crashes, rewarding those who maintain discipline. By resisting the urge to act on short-term fears, you increase your chances of benefiting from the inevitable upswing.

Stay calm, be diversified, and avoid letting short-term anxiety guide your decisions. Focus on long-term growth, and the market will reward your discipline.

THE DANGER OF FOLLOWING HOT TIPS

Always verify investment tips before diving in. Even when advice comes from trusted sources like friends, family, or financial advisors, it's essential to do your own research. Blindly following hot tips can be dangerous. Why? Because those offering advice may have good intentions, but they can still be wrong, and ultimately, you are the one who bears the consequences.

I learned this lesson the hard way. A friend once shared a hot tip that led to some initial gains, but the next recommendation resulted in a major loss. Watching my hard-earned money disappear was frustrating, and it was a harsh reminder of the dangers of relying on others without doing my own homework.

That experience completely changed my approach to investing. I realized that, no matter how well meaning the advice, I had to trust my instincts and do my own research to truly take control of my financial future.

THE HIDDEN RISK OF COMPLEXITY

When faced with complex investments, if you don't fully understand the risks, it's best not to proceed. Simplicity often protects wealth more effectively than complexity. Let me explain.

If an investment seems too complicated, it's best to pause and evaluate. Many people make costly mistakes chasing bigger returns through investments they don't fully understand.

Simple investments, like index funds or real estate, may not seem as exciting, but they come with significantly less risk and fewer chances for things to go wrong. Stick to what you understand—because, while complexity may offer the allure of large rewards, it often conceals risks that can derail your financial progress.

THE HIDDEN DANGER OF DEBT

Using debt can amplify your gains, but it also increases the risk of significant losses when conditions take a turn for the worse. Borrowing money to invest, whether through margin accounts in the stock market or loans for real estate or business ventures, may seem manageable during favorable conditions, but when circumstances change unexpectedly, the risks are magnified.

That's what makes debt so dangerous—it can lead to disaster when things don't go as planned.

I once had a client who used a substantial amount of debt to invest in stocks. As his portfolio surged, he grew confident, feeling as if he were making easy money. But when the market fell, his losses were devastating.

Another client took out a large loan to expand his business just before a recession hit. When sales in his business dried up, he couldn't keep up with the loan payments, and his business went bankrupt.

In both cases, debt didn't just magnify returns—it exposed them to greater risk, leading to financial ruin when things went wrong.

Avoid excess debt. While it may seem like a tempting shortcut to amplify gains, it introduces more risk that can undermine your financial progress.

THE IMPORTANCE OF INSURANCE AND PREPAREDNESS

Disasters are unpredictable, but you can protect yourself by ensuring you're adequately insured. Whether it's health, home, or liability coverage, the right insurance can safeguard you from financial ruin.

Without proper coverage, a single health crisis, car accident, or natural disaster could wipe out years of financial progress.

Don't cut corners on insurance. Take time to review your policies and ensure you have the coverage you need.

AVOID LENDING MONEY

Some of the hardest financial setbacks come from those closest to us. Lending money to friends or family may feel like the right thing to do, but it often backfires both financially and emotionally.

I once lent $10,000 to a close friend who promised to repay me within a week. That week turned into months, and our friendship deteriorated. The stress of asking for my money back and the frustration of not being repaid ruined our relationship. In the end, I lost both the money and the friendship.

Now, when a friend asks for money, I offer what I can as a gift, not a loan. If they don't accept, that's their choice. By giving instead of lending, I avoid the stress of unpaid debts and preserve the relationship.

OVERCOMING SETBACKS ON YOUR WEALTH JOURNEY

Financial setbacks can be mentally exhausting. Watching your hard-earned wealth decline can trigger stress and frustration, making it feel like all your effort was in vain. It's easy to lose confidence in your financial decisions during these times, but setbacks are a natural part of the wealth-building process.

What truly matters isn't avoiding every challenge, but how well prepared and resilient you are when they arise.

Resilience means having the right mindset and strategies to recover when adversity strikes. Building wealth isn't about a smooth, uninterrupted path. It's about navigating the inevitable obstacles with preparation and a long-term perspective. By reinforcing solid financial habits, you position yourself to weather financial storms and emerge stronger on the other side.

7

CAPITALIZE ON WEALTH OPPORTUNITIES

As you work toward building wealth, you'll encounter opportunities that can dramatically accelerate your progress. The key is to be prepared and ready to act because these opportunities are often brief and can disappear quickly.

In this chapter, I'll share examples of opportunities to help you identify and seize them.

STOCK MARKET CRASHES

Most people fear stock market crashes because the panic and uncertainty can feel overwhelming. However, for those with a long-term mindset, a market crash is a golden opportunity to buy high-quality stocks at a discount.

Take the crash in 2020 as an example. While many investors sold off their stocks in a panic, I took the opposite approach and increased my buying activity. I didn't make reckless decisions or go all-in, but I did invest more heavily.

Within months, the market recovered, and four years later, many of the stocks I purchased had risen by 300%. These weren't speculative startups; they were stable, billion-dollar companies.

It's important to maintain some cash or liquid assets so you're ready to take advantage of market crashes. But don't let too much of your capital sit idle—otherwise, inflation will erode its value. Make sure your cash reserves are earning interest or providing some return to offset inflation. Avoid panic selling and focus on quality investments.

Crashes are temporary, but the stock market will recover and continue to grow over the long term. Stay calm, buy strategically, and hold with patience.

REAL ESTATE CRASHES

Like the stock market, real estate crashes can offer incredible opportunities to buy valuable assets at reduced prices. I learned this firsthand during the Great Recession of 2007, but at the time, I wasn't in a position to take advantage of it. I lacked the money, assets, and credit necessary to make a move. Still, I vowed to be ready for the next opportunity.

That chance came in 2020 when the pandemic caused a downturn in certain urban real estate markets. Properties in highly desirable locations were suddenly available at significant discounts. This time, I was prepared. I purchased an investment property at a price that would have been unimaginable just a few months earlier, and its value has increased significantly since then.

From my experience, here's my advice: Don't buy a property based solely on price. In real estate, location is everything. A reduced price on a bad property or in an undesirable area is no bargain. Even in a downturn, focus on locations with strong future potential, as real estate values often take time to increase meaningfully.

EARLY ADOPTION

Opportunities aren't limited to market downturns—being an early adopter in emerging technologies or industries can also yield tremendous financial rewards. You don't need to be the smartest or hardest-working person—sometimes, being early is enough.

I first heard about Bitcoin through my clients when it was priced around $700. As a tax professional, I had to learn about cryptocurrency because my clients were asking tax-related questions about Bitcoin and Ethereum. After researching, I decided to invest. Looking back, it's incredible how much wealth I accumulated by simply being early.

The key to early adoption is patience. Just because you're ahead of the curve doesn't mean the rewards will come overnight. The technology, ideas, or assets you invest in might take years to reach their full potential. But if you've done your research and believe in their growth, waiting for the long-term payoff can lead to extraordinary returns.

It's important to keep an open mind when you're exposed to new technologies or ideas. If something seems promising, take the time to investigate it. Early adoption can lead to significant financial rewards, but it requires curiosity and a willingness to explore new opportunities.

CAREER OPPORTUNITIES

Wealth-building opportunities also exist in your career. Whether it's switching companies, expanding your business, or starting something new, these moves can significantly boost your income.

Early in my career, I was stuck in a miserable job at a billion-dollar company. The hours were long, the pay was mediocre, and the work environment was toxic. After three years of waiting for the right moment to leave, I noticed a gap in the market—a shortage of skilled tax professionals in my area.

Taking a leap of faith, I started my own tax practice, which turned out to be one of the best decisions of my life.

As my business grew, I had opportunities to hire employees, offer additional services, and expand into new markets. Each time I acted on these, both my income and wealth increased. What began as a solo practice evolved into a thriving business—all because I recognized and pursued career opportunities when they arose.

ADAPTING TO UNLOCK NEW OPPORTUNITIES

Not all opportunities will align perfectly with your current plans or expectations. Sometimes, building wealth requires a shift in direction, new strategies, or a different way of thinking. Being adaptable means staying open to adjusting your approach when necessary—whether that's shifting investment strategies or taking on new roles in your career that you hadn't originally considered.

In my own career, adaptability was a key factor in my success. When I realized I couldn't serve all my clients on my own, I hired employees and expanded my business. When social media became a powerful platform, I adjusted my strategy and started making videos, which turned into a huge success. Each of these moments required flexibility and a willingness to move in a new direction.

While it's important to stay focused on long-term goals, being adaptable can unlock unexpected opportunities for growth. The ability to pivot when needed can be just as valuable as careful planning.

UNCOVERING HIDDEN OPPORTUNITIES

Wealth-building opportunities aren't always obvious. Sometimes, they emerge from everyday moments or seemingly unrelated experiences. Recognizing these invisible opportunities can lead to unexpected financial gains.

Hobbies or side projects, even if unrelated to your career or investing, can unexpectedly turn into wealth-building ventures. I've seen clients transform hobbies into successful businesses or make valuable connections through shared interests, leading to financial success they hadn't anticipated.

Stay curious and open to possibilities in all areas of life. Some of the best opportunities come from the least expected places. By staying alert, you can turn these moments into meaningful opportunities for wealth-building.

PURSUING CALCULATED RISKS FOR GREATER REWARDS

Every opportunity, whether in the stock market, real estate, or your career, involves some level of risk. Taking a calculated risk can lead to significant rewards. The key is to minimize your downside, pursue risks where the odds are in your favor, and never risk an amount that could cripple your financial well-being.

For example, when the S&P 500 plunged during the pandemic, I knew the market could fall further, but it was unlikely to hit zero. With the risk-reward balance skewed in my favor, I invested more heavily in the stock market.

Similarly, when I started my tax practice, I minimized risk by keeping initial costs low. I began in my small apartment with no employees. As the business grew, I moved to a shared office, then a private office, and eventually hired staff—always expanding only when I was financially secure enough to handle the next step.

EMBRACING OPPORTUNITIES ON YOUR WEALTH JOURNEY

On your wealth-building journey, opportunities will come in many forms. The key is to be prepared, stay adaptable, and allow long-term rewards to develop. By spotting opportunities and acting with patience and foresight, you can accelerate your path to financial success.

8

NEVER STOP LEARNING

The greatest investment you can make is in yourself. Continuous learning isn't just beneficial; it's essential for long-term success. Expanding your knowledge and developing new skills not only enriches your life but also unlocks new opportunities and boosts your earning potential.

Learning doesn't have to be limited to finance or career-related subjects. You should expand your knowledge in any area that interests you, even if it seems unrelated to wealth-building. You never know when a new skill or knowledge will intersect with your financial journey and create unexpected opportunities.

HOW LEARNING SPANISH LED TO AN UNEXPECTED DISCOVERY

Let me share a personal experience. My parents immigrated to the United States from South Korea, and I was born and raised in the US.

In my thirties, I decided to learn Spanish. I really didn't have a good reason to. I didn't have any Spanish-speaking friends or clients, and I wasn't traveling much. But I thought learning a new language would be interesting, and I had nothing better to do during my train commute to work, so I decided to start learning.

I stayed committed, and after a few months, I reached an intermediate level. One day, on a whim, I made a short video about Spanish slang and uploaded it to YouTube, sharing it on social media. I made the video just for fun, without any expectations, but to my surprise, it got thousands of views, and people started subscribing to my channel. The positive feedback motivated me to keep improving my Spanish.

Seeing the success of that video sparked an idea: If a fun video like this could gain so much attention, why not create educational content about taxes on YouTube to boost my business? So I did—and it worked!

Had I never learned Spanish, I might never have ventured into social media, and you wouldn't be reading this book today. That one skill put me on an entirely new path to financial success.

CORE LEARNING AREAS TO ELEVATE YOUR SUCCESS

Success involves ongoing growth in several important areas. Here are some key areas you should consider improving to boost both your personal and financial success. By focusing on these, you can strengthen your abilities and unlock new opportunities for long-term growth.

LEARN MORE ABOUT YOUR CRAFT

Mastering your field doesn't just improve your efficiency—it elevates your long-term earning potential. Whether you're employed or self-employed, continually improving your professional skills will increase your value and help you command higher pay.

LEARN TO INVEST SMARTER

The more you understand about investing, the better equipped you'll be to grow your wealth. You don't need to be an expert in every asset class, but focusing on one or two—such as stocks, real estate, or bonds—will help you recognize opportunities others might miss.

LEARN FROM YOUR MISTAKES

Mistakes are inevitable, but they're powerful lessons for growth. The key is to see setbacks not as failures, but as valuable feedback that gets you closer to success. Every mistake strengthens your ability to make smarter decisions in the future.

LEARN TO STRENGTHEN YOUR PEOPLE SKILLS

Technical knowledge alone isn't enough. Understanding people and managing relationships is just as important. Developing your communication, emotional intelligence, and leadership skills will make you more effective—whether you're negotiating deals, managing teams, or marketing.

LEARN MORE ABOUT YOURSELF

Self-awareness is a critical yet often overlooked aspect of personal growth. Many people go through life without realizing their natural talents, which prevents them from reaching their full potential. The more you understand your strengths, weaknesses, and motivations, the better equipped you'll be to tackle challenges and seize new opportunities.

LEARN NEW HOBBIES

Exploring new interests can lead to unexpected opportunities. Hobbies aren't just for relaxation—they can open doors to new income streams or business ventures. Even if they don't result in direct financial gains, hobbies boost creativity, enhance problem-solving skills, and positively shape your mindset.

LEARN BY TRAVELING

Travel is an invaluable teacher. It broadens your perspective, exposes you to new ideas, and reveals opportunities you may not have noticed before. Stepping outside your usual environment often sparks fresh insights that can benefit both your personal and financial life.

Travel doesn't just introduce you to new cultures—it expands your thinking and fosters adaptability. Whether you're interacting with people from diverse backgrounds or learning about different markets, travel sharpens your ability to discover opportunities beyond your everyday surroundings.

CONTINUOUS LEARNING AS A LIFESTYLE

Continuous learning isn't just a one-time effort—it's a lifestyle choice. It's about cultivating the habit of questioning, improving, and expanding your knowledge and skills. Avoid falling into autopilot mode. Make a conscious effort to learn, focusing on incremental improvements in every aspect of your life.

These small, consistent changes compound over time, much like investing. Each new skill you acquire and lesson you learn contributes to both your personal and financial growth. Think of yourself as a character in a video game, leveling up with each new skill and piece of knowledge. The more you learn, the more powerful you become, making it easier to achieve financial success.

9

ROUTINES THAT BUILD WEALTH

To accelerate your path to wealth, developing a routine is essential. Without one, maintaining consistency becomes difficult, and progress can stall.

Just like an exercise routine keeps you fit, a structured approach to managing your time and finances ensures steady progress toward your financial goals.

A routine helps you focus on the right tasks, minimize distractions, and build good habits through repetition. Whether it's daily, weekly, or monthly, a well-designed routine instills discipline and ensures you consistently dedicate time to moving closer to your objectives.

ROUTINES FOR THE SELF-EMPLOYED

For the self-employed, having a routine is even more essential because you don't have a boss who is supervising you.

While the freedom of self-employment is a tremendous advantage, it can become a drawback if time isn't managed effectively. A lack of structure often leads to distractions, missed deadlines, and underperformance. A well-structured routine provides the framework needed to make the most of your time while still enjoying the benefits of self-employment.

FLEXIBILITY AND AVOIDING BURNOUT

While routines are vital, it's just as important to stay flexible. Planned breaks are key to avoiding burnout and maintaining productivity. These pauses allow you to recharge and return with renewed focus.

Personally, I follow my routine as closely as possible because it keeps me disciplined, helps me break bad habits, and builds good ones. Whether it's work, exercise, or learning new skills, my routine supports steady progress. However, there's value and benefits of breaking the routine when needed.

DON'T OVERLOOK THESE ELEMENTS IN YOUR ROUTINE

Your routine shouldn't just focus on primary tasks. It should also make room for learning, experimentation, and even failure. Failure is a natural part of growth. You can't improve without trying new things, taking calculated risks, and learning from mistakes. Build a routine that allows time for trial and error, and you'll see growth both personally and financially.

It's also essential to set measurable goals within your routine. These might include reaching a specific financial target or broader objectives such as making progress or maintaining a certain skill level. The key is to have a way to track your progress so you can monitor your growth and adjust your routine as needed.

STREAMLINE WEALTH-BUILDING WITH AUTOMATION

One of the most effective routines for building wealth is automating your savings and investments. Each time you get paid, set up automatic transfers to your retirement, brokerage, or savings accounts. This practice of "paying yourself first" ensures that a portion of your income is always directed toward growing your wealth.

I used to struggle with consistency when managing my finances. I'd save one month and then get off track the next. Once I set up automatic transfers, it became much easier to stay consistent. Over time, those automated contributions added up, and I began to see real progress.

Automation removes the temptation to spend money that should be saved. By consistently setting aside funds, you create a system that steadily brings you closer to financial freedom.

ACCOUNTABILITY: THE KEY TO STAYING CONSISTENT

Accountability is crucial for maintaining routines. Don't rely on willpower alone. Create systems to keep yourself on track. Whether it's using a simple checklist, tracking your progress with apps, or involving a friend or mentor to hold you accountable, external systems can be powerful tools.

For instance, I use a daily checklist to track the tasks I need to complete. Having a clear list keeps me focused and ensures I stay accountable.

THE DANGER OF OVERAMBITIOUS ROUTINES

One common mistake is creating a routine that's too ambitious. Overloading your schedule can lead to burnout and frustration, making it more likely that you'll abandon the routine altogether.

Another pitfall is getting discouraged if you don't see immediate results. Routines are about steady, incremental progress, not overnight transformations. It may take weeks or even months to notice significant changes, so it's important to stay patient and trust the process.

REDUCE DECISION FATIGUE WITH STRUCTURED ROUTINES

Routines do more than build discipline. They free up mental energy by reducing decision fatigue. Every day is filled with countless decisions, both big and small. Having a routine in place takes care of many of these choices and leaves you with more focus for what truly matters. This makes it easier to stay on course as you work toward your financial goals.

PERSONALIZING YOUR ROUTINE

Your routine should be tailored to your unique circumstances and goals. You don't need to copy the routine of someone successful—what works for them might not work for you.

For example, just because a Fortune 500 CEO wakes up at 4:00 a.m. doesn't mean you need to. What truly matters is how you use your time, not when you wake up. We all have the same twenty-four hours in a day. It's how you make the most of them that counts. Create a routine that works for you.

COMMIT TO YOUR ROUTINE AND BUILD YOUR WEALTH

Routines are ultimately about building consistency and creating a clear path toward your goals. They shouldn't feel restrictive; instead, they should empower you by simplifying daily decisions and keeping you focused on what truly matters.

As you refine your routine, remember that progress is made one step at a time. Start small, stay flexible, and adjust as needed. Whether you're automating your savings, setting measurable goals, or holding yourself accountable, these habits will compound over time, steadily moving you closer to financial freedom.

Design a routine that fits your life and commit to it. Each day that you follow through on your plan, you'll be building not just your wealth but a strong foundation for long-term success.

10

THE DECISION TO BECOME WEALTHY

Now that you have the recipe for building wealth and achieving financial freedom, there's one final step: taking action. Knowledge alone won't get you there—it's the daily decisions and actions that will shape your financial future.

Think of it like improving your fitness. You know the basics—eat healthier and exercise regularly—but real results come from consistently pushing through excuses and staying committed. Building wealth works the same way. Every decision either strengthens your financial future or holds you back.

CULTIVATE A RESISTANT MENTALITY

To stay on track, you need a resistant mentality. This means staying focused on your goals, even when temptations and challenges arise. Building wealth requires unwavering commitment to your long-term objectives, even when distractions seem more appealing.

Keep your vision front and center—whether it's financial independence, security for your family, or the freedom to live on your own terms.

START NOW, REGARDLESS OF YOUR SITUATION

The good news is that it doesn't matter where you're starting from. Whether you're in debt or earning modestly, the key is to start now. Every day you delay is a missed opportunity.

I started with very little, just like many others, but deliberate steps and commitment changed my financial future. You can do the same.

If you're unsure where to begin, start by tracking your income and expenses. From there, focus on increasing your income, managing your spending, and investing the difference.

BUILD MOMENTUM WITH SMALL WINS

Small victories fuel your progress. Whether it's saving your first $1,000 or making your first investment in an index fund, these early wins reinforce your decision to build wealth. Progress may seem slow at first, but consistency is what matters. Like compound interest, today's small actions will accumulate and lead to greater financial gains over time.

WEALTH IS A CHOICE

Becoming wealthy is a choice you make every day. Challenges will come, but by staying focused and resilient, you can overcome them.

Wealth-building is about prioritizing your financial future and following through with intention. You're either moving closer to your goals or further away. The choice is yours.

Start today. Take control of your financial future and commit to the actions that will lead you to wealth and freedom.

What will you choose today?

DID YOU ENJOY THIS BOOK?

Thank you for reading *The Book of Wealth: 10 Steps to Financial Freedom.* I sincerely hope it helps guide you on your journey toward financial freedom.

If you found value in this book, I'd greatly appreciate it if you could take a moment to leave a review on Amazon.

I read every review and truly appreciate your feedback—it not only motivates me but also helps others discover the book.

Thank you for your support!

Made in United States
Troutdale, OR
01/16/2025

28036662R00051